WILDFLOWERS RISING IN THE BONEYARD

James N. Wicklund

My father intended to dedicate this volume to Linda Jenewein, his life partner for many of his autumn years.

As his health declined, he did not finish the planning for this book, including completing the dedication. I would not dare to try to guess what my father might have written, so I can only speak for myself and my family in expressing our gratitude for the love and happiness Linda shared with Dad.

– Joel Wicklund

CONTENTS

Introduction	*vii*
Accidents Happen	1
Act Three	2
Adverbials	4
Amazing Grace	5
Assisted Living	6
Au Naturel	7
Audience	9
Devoutly to Be Wished	10
Encryption	11
Entrance Song	12
Evolution	15
Giving Four Fingers	17
Giving Gifts	18
Glances	19
A Hermit's Life with Others	20
Hunting	21
Hypotheticals	22
In the Details	23
Instead	26
Legacy	27
The Loudness of the Leaving	28
Mail	29
Miscellanea II	30
Missing the Early Show	31
My Turn	32
Mysteries / Research	33
Narratives	35
Oh Say Can You See	38
On the Morning of Departure	39
Or Not to Be	40

Role   41

Rubrics of Gratitude   42

Schläft ein Lied   46

Show Biz   47

Simulation   48

Sonnet on an Occasional Visit   49

Stripping Lesson   50

Time for an Anniversary   51

Tremors   52

Turning   53

Unheard   55

Vanishing Points   56

Vigil   57

Villanelle Pour Mon Amour   58

Wildflowers Rising in the Boneyard   59

Without Gravity   61

Introduction

My father was a teacher and school administrator, and his career in education lasted almost 40 years. For an even longer period than that, however, he was a poet.

After his passing, I found files of his poetry going back to the 1950s. In the decades where raising a family and his job occupied so much of his time, I'm not sure how prolific he was (we were certainly left with a much larger body of work from his retirement years), but it's clear he always saw poetry as passionate avocation, not a mere hobby.

He was modest about sharing his writing until he self-published a volume of his work, *Notes Found Scratched on a Bald Spot*, in 2010. That book, dedicated to my late mother Patricia (who had died two years earlier) and their children, was presented to us as a "family heirloom." But while it included poems written about us and many poems and short pieces of prose drawn from a lifetime of memories, I think Dad was just slightly disingenuous about the reach he desired for the book.

Don't misunderstand me; he truly wanted our family and his closest friends to have that book to treasure in the present and to remember him by when he passed. However, I also think this writer who had honed his craft for decades wanted his book out in the world, even if only in a very modest fashion. He made more expensive self-publishing options than loved ones would have expected for a personal gift, and he ensured he obtained an ISBN code and made the book available on Amazon.* He also paid to have many more copies printed than he needed for his stated intended group of recipients. In short, he took great pride in his work and, though he was too humble and/or insecure to market it heavily, I think he quietly hoped others beyond his circle of loved ones might, by chance, discover it.

I am not deeply steeped in poetry and certainly no expert on it — and of course, as his son, I am deeply biased — but I think Dad was justified in hoping to reach a wider base of readers. Of course, opinions on poetry, like all arts, are subjective; but I don't think the thoughtfulness, precision and emotion of my father's best work are deniable. He studied and knew the many forms, thought seriously about when and how to break those forms, and he had a distinctive voice.

I believe his growing pride in his writing (even if he rarely admitted to it), was one reason he decided he wanted to publish a second volume of his work as his health started to fade. But this wasn't simply a writer's ego; he also had something to say. And, with his personal finish line in sight, a lot of what he had to say was about aging and death.

Death was by no means a new subject for my father. On the one hand, Jim Wicklund was one of the most upbeat people you could ever hope to meet. He embraced friends, family and the worlds of travel, the arts and culture with absolute enthusiasm. Nobody enjoyed a good laugh like Dad, whether triggered by a brilliant joke or a groan-inducing pun. He found so much so funny, from the sophistication of Oscar Wilde to the broadest physical comedy (*Weekend at Bernie's* was a favorite). And in his hopes for his children, his desire that we all find joy in life was often strongly stated.

But my father also had a solemn, melancholy side. Loss was no stranger to him and as a one-time seminarian-turned-atheist (or at least agnostic, as he considered the possibility of a higher power in some conversations), a serious contemplation of his mortality started young and continued until his passing. Even when he was only in his forties, I can recall him telling us, his children, how we had to be prepared for "when I pop," as he comically put it. I don't think he saw himself living to a very old age, especially after being diagnosed with some heart issues in his early fifties.

He did, however, surpass his expectations, living until 86 and enjoying a long and vibrant retirement, even allowing for the heartbreaks and losses that inevitably come with age. Still, "the end" was never far from his mind.

Not all the poems in this volume are about death or aging, by any means. There are also poems about love, passion, family dynamics, politics, regrets, hopes, dreams and more. But finality is a constant presence — usually on the periphery when not the main focus of the writing. Finality, though, comes in many flavors here, from the wrenching remembrances of "Vigil" to the irreverent optimism of the work that gives this book its title, "Wildflowers Rising in the Boneyard."

Though my father was compiling poems for this volume before he died, I need to emphasize this collection remains something of a best guess of his intentions. There were several variances to navigate: different edits on some poems (without dates to know which were the earlier or preferred versions); hand-written, in-progress works stuffed into a folder with completed poems; physical versus digital files, etc. He left a couple of directional notes in emails and I've tried to be true to the spirit of those notes, but I can't claim this is exactly the book he would have delivered had he lived a little longer. I hope it is close to the mark.

Dad was also very interested in different physical constructions of poetry. While he adored and practiced the most traditional forms, he enjoyed playing with varying indentations of text and even changes in line spacing. In some cases, I know his choice of single versus double versus 1.5 line spacing was very much intentional. In others…well, maybe he just forgot he used 1.5 spacing last time around? Not wanting to guess and throw off his intentions, I have kept each poem as it was spaced originally.

I want to thank my siblings Pete Wicklund, Karen Widdowson and Germaine Clarno; my sister-in-law Ruby Shemanske; and Linda Jenewein, my father's life partner in his final years, for trusting me in those instances when subjective choices were necessary and for giving me the privilege of compiling and securing a publishing platform for this book. I also want to thank my wife, Jennifer Worrell, for providing a valuable second set of eyes in proofreading the contents.

We all miss my father tremendously. Although it has been a while since his passing, his absence is felt every day. Our family's world is the lesser for him not being here and I dare say the world of poetry is the lesser for him not being here…even if most of that vast world is entirely unaware of his output.

I don't harbor any fantasies that my father will gain wide, posthumous recognition as a poet. In an art form where even acclaimed poets work in relative obscurity, that is beyond unrealistic. What I do hope for — and what I think my father hoped for with his efforts on his first book — is that it reaches *some* new readers as the years go by…those who will know him only as a writer. I hope this book will be found in tiny but wonderful ways…a random online discovery, a copy sold on consignment in an independent bookstore, or one left in one of those charming birdhouse-like "free libraries" in a residential neighborhood.

Whether it reaches 50, 500 or 5,000 readers doesn't matter too much to me, so long as within whatever modest audience it finds, there is some true appreciation. The idea that even one complete stranger might stumble across this book, read it and think, "This James Wicklund is a hell of a poet…why isn't he better known?" delights me…and I think it would delight Dad.

If you are that appreciative reader, thank you.

-- Joel Wicklund

* Though currently no longer available on Amazon, limited copies of *Notes Found Scratched on a Bald Spot* are available through **jameswicklund.com**, where you can also find more of James Wicklund's poetry.

ACCIDENTS HAPPEN

Planets collide.
Atoms collide.
Genes collide.

Life is constant collision.

An embrace is a calculated crash.

ACT THREE

Bowing to Robert Browning

This doesn't feel right!

It never did, even at auditions.

There's been a grave mistake.

I was supposed to be a noticed player,

    not a faceless walk-on.

I thought my role was to be the lead's main support –

    a kind of Horatio with my own appeal

    and my own poetry.

But the audience's eyes never turned on my entrance –

    the hero was still reciting,

    ranting really!

    emoting so effusively

    that only *his* words were heard,

    only *his* presence noticed.

Why were they so enrapt?

    His lines were a measly, mousy complaint,

    whereas I offered strength to his crumbling soul.

    And I spoke in eloquent, winning words!

    That's in the script, you know!

    I should have been admired,

    not simply *endured* by the audience

    until *he* spoke again!

Oh, yes, the director gave me my entrances and exits,

    my limited gestures, my sparse movements,

    but no chances to spotlight my character –

    no stage time to shine, as I could have.

There'll be the curtain call soon,

    and the few scattered hand-claps when I take my bow

    will be drowned in repeated "Bravos"

    and in thunderous applause for *him*.

    And he will bow oh *so* grandly!

ADVERBIALS

All that you are

since you became my now

and my here

and my everywhere

Is all that I am.

Your thens

and your whens

and your untils

are now my nows –

my how soons

and my every time

and my all the time

and my ever yours.

AMAZING GRACE

Starting softly, shuffling humbly, then stately

into a grandeur beyond one's person,

the rhyming angels were swaying

as they sang solemn verses,

"et cum spiritu tu - toot tooting"

in a choral wave of wispy gowns

and the deepest bass notes of the organ

throbbed in a vaulted sound

that swirled, twisting the bodies

in the pews.

Candles flickered, fluid tallow melting

with the scents of incensed, perfumed perspiration

and joy's entrance had been felt,

sweated, melted, tasted and breathed.

ASSISTED LIVING

Each of us carries along a kind of tank

through which we breathe the days we live,

tethered to a measured supply of succor

that pumps whatever remains

through plastic tubing that bends and sweats

as we suck in what we think we wish for.

Fearing deprivation,

deeply devouring,

we fill perforated lungs

with promise of heartbeats,

of sensing,

of continuing awareness --

feasting on mere air.

AU NATUREL

One would have to call it a public bath.

After all, it was out there in full view

    of anyone looking out the window

    or passing by.

In the small rain-puddle collected atop

    an iron sewer cover,

a half-dozen or more sparrows spread their wings,

    bobbed their heads,

    and splashed water over and under their bodies,

not for pleasure, it seemed,

but because it was time for bathing.

There was no chirping for attention,

no posturing or even preening,

no intentional display of bodies.

Nothing seemed excessive, or unnecessary,

    or inappropriate,

even though the birds were obviously uncovered,

assuming that their feathers were,

    like our body hair, part of their bodies,

    without which their natures would be changed significantly.

    There didn't seem to be any covert peeking at others

    comparing beak-length or wing-spread.

The baths were delicate and brief,

after which each naked bird flew off quickly,

intent on finding far more to life than public bathing,

    or the viewing thereof.

AUDIENCE

I teased myself into dreaming
of marble permanence despite
the lost limbs and faded faces
of statues chiseled long ago.

And I'd embrace such stony state
if I could still search, with flattened,
wind-sculpted eyes, past missing nose,
with solemn jaw somewhat crumbled,

the roaring of the rushing sea,
the floating closeness of the waves,
the horizon's deep distances,
the gliding flights of the seagulls,
the crossings of the moon-lit clouds,
the continuing of the life.

DEVOUTLY TO BE WISHED

What I want to believe
       I cannot make be.
Elaborate dreams are fantasies.
Even urgent desire
       will not bring satisfaction –
       only the real is true.

A beast in pursuit
       can win capture
       – a lesser prize –
but what he caught he must consume.
His nature must be proved.

I can only embrace what I hold.
       Let me taste your truth.
       My beast must be fed, as well.

ENCRYPTION

There are languages found to be useless,

    desperately discarded,

    strewn in the dark alleys of thought.

There are moments

    when we don't allow the voice to speak.

We have words

    that no one has ever heard.

    Agreement gets a nod.

      Tears express hurt.

        Anger is swallowed.

We stand mute in horror's presence.

    We stare into emptiness

      when we have no answer to give,

      there in the dark, silent alleys of thought.

ENTRANCE SONG

Waves of frothy violins drifting from ceiling speakers

abruptly stop in momentary, detached silence.

A lullaby in music-box chimes softly follows,

proudly announcing to the hospital's world the birth of a child.

In thick upholstered chairs in the waiting areas of each department,

patients sit patiently, their attention caught by the chimes.

A mother tries to soothe a bandaged girl "Oh listen, honey,

a baby has just been born!"

A tank-topped man in his twenties,

head wrapped in a bloodied, sweaty strip of cloth,

reluctantly listens,

timidly wringing anger from his greasy hands.

An older couple, sitting opposite each other,

disappointments familiar,

glimpse grudgingly across their distance

wondering separately, "Why? Why another?"

Someone recalls pictures he had seen —

a child's head pulled through the moist tunnel between the woman's legs

seemingly squinting at the light,

then crying out his arrival, his shock, his needs!

A saddened woman of forty

remembers kisses hindering the sight

of fingers stroking anxiously,

passion beginning its crescendo.

A man lonely in his thoughts

sees the dewy lips opening

like morning blossoms

before the pulsing, silken flow.

An old man, his unaided ears deaf to the music,

wonders why the woman who smiled at the chimes

as she looked his way

turned abruptly when he winked.

He can't hear the simple lullaby, the memory of lush passage,

the chiming of treasured entering and exiting,

the lusting and the liberating

in rushing, shouting streams.

EVOLUTION

Leaving gurgling sweetness to scream adolescent anger,

scorning deep-felt certainty for insolent disdain,

mourning loss to demanding pleasure,

A person continues.

It's said nothing stays the same.

Those were not stages, not even moments.

They were times unmeasured:

sorrow, joy, promise, ignominy, foolishness, futility.

They were entirely all the now when they were,

and are every then in its endless now,

the sweet and the salt, the softness and the grit,

the singing and the moaning,

the perfume and the reek of every anything,

all the passage and each part,

continuing hurt and constant healing.

If chance allows an old man to feel warmth in remembering arms,

taste longing in his recalling loins,

taste love on his revived tongue;

when promise is restored,

there is not a then remembered but a now newly come,

a cleaving closeness, an enclosing embrace, a breathless body,

a presence possessing as fiercely as long-lived arms will tolerate.

It's said that nothing stays the same,

but now seems what as it was:

known chasm and familiar spasm find ever-new orchesis, the pulsing part

like the lowering delving scale of an ancient organ just-now heard,

the song's downward surging,

then the increasing, the organized, essence of chorded erupting,

and the young-fresh refusal of <u>any</u> when of inevitable change.

GIVING FOUR FINGERS

When Pythagoras proudly proposed his plausible theorem,

proving his prominence,

his prim proficiency,

he presented the order of,

the right-ness of,

certain triangulated areas.

Though significantly later than

the Babylonians and the Egyptians,

the Chinese and the Indians,

even the miscellaneous Mesopotamians,

his more proper pronouncement

was presumed *probatum est* (as Romans would later phrase it),

truly true, indeed *Western* – a more assuring cachet.

A religious man, Pythagoras sacrificed a bull to *Tetraktys*,

divine digital basis of reason, argument, peace and justice.

To this day, *bull* remains the basis for Western civilization.

GIVING GIFTS

Peace, as if it came from somewhere else,
was to be prayed for, sent for.
But peace is always here,
buried under the detritus of other concerns —
busy-ness of needs,
insistence of pain,
dominance of pleasure and exhaustion.

But I can unbury it, free its stream,
let it shower my presence.
I'll share its limitless rush with you
and you share yours with me.

May peace be always with you.

GLANCES

I sat reading, then glanced at the cat
      stretched on the floor,
      who glanced back at me
      as if to confirm our connection.

That is what you and I do as well.

There are no words,
      no touches,
      no letters,
      no calls,
      no e-mails or public broadcasts
that confirm our truths
      more precisely,
      more nakedly evident
      than such glances.

A HERMIT'S LIFE WITH OTHERS

Here I am, still in the world of someone else

On the day of departure.

All the things that seemed so different,

    Exotic or just interesting,

    Strange or just new,

Now feel familiar, as if I were truly a native here.

But the arrangements for leaving have been made,

    Non-exchangeable and non-refundable,

And the prearranged transportation will arrive momentarily.

I've forgotten what home looks like.

HUNTING

Among countless half-shells
washed up by the surf,
birds called "Oyster Catchers"
run through wet sand,
long beaks probing,
seeking remaining shreds
of former residents,

like hungry derelicts
intently scavenging
fast-food wrappings
in trash bins
behind condominiums.

HYPOTHETICALS

Maybe there *is* a higher power after all,
some forceful canon that decrees joy is momentary,
that good life must be abbreviated,
that presence is merely the past just begun;
that pleasure is but a breath in time,
that time defines our life, measures our love.

And maybe there *is* a terrible insistence
that misfortune is not evil,
that we are not fully alive,
that we are continuing to die.

But we learn, over time,
that time is our hope to avoid change –
that time is our dreamt wishes.

We're taught acceptance has rewards,
that carrying burdens is heroic,
and that (surprise!) we *do* live happily forever!
What do you know?
We've been fooled.
Isn't that something!

IN THE DETAILS

There's always the rush to buy music
       to be played again some time,
reminded celebrations,
songs scenting the air
       retelling myths, softening the details.
       Images of fallen leaves or hills of snow or city streets
          course through the veins of reminiscence
             selecting appropriate sentiments.

Our memories are scotch-taped
       to lives that might-have-happened in sun-shiny songs.
We happily adhere to those joyous abstractions,
         distractions of the should-have-been.

But there's the other end of it,
       the small print on the back label of living,
       without the colors and the lush logos on the front,
       without glittered ribbons that hold unopened surprises,
       without expectations of satisfactions finally fulfilled;
       without realizing a this-can't-be-true moment,
or hearing applause for an at-long-last-noticed deed,
and without winning the lottery at just-the-right-time.

After all the ardent awkwardness of life's early groping
        and even after maturity's generous gush of release
        and the softer breathing of later years,
all the falderal finally passes into a somewhat pleasured peace;
but not until there was an understanding of it,
        the once-upon-a-time-ness of it,
        the tears and the fears before the happily-ever-after,
        the often-occurrence of a once-in-a-lifetime,
        all the situations and all the persons,
        the placing-some-aside and nuzzling-others-closely,
        a culling of the littered lives created by circumstance,
                some tossed away from caring,
                some caressed for a time, until,
                        like faded photos,
                memories reach the album's last page;

        like a clock almost unwound, feebly ticking.
                recalling motions of a slow-dance tune,
        or like sounds from scratched shards of broken records,
                        pieces of the air breathed once;

        and then the silent awareness of life's long brevity,

all the give and hate of it,

all the love and take of it;

25

and the quiet, dusk-arrived discovery that

that was then,

a very long ago then.

INSTEAD

We cry for our own death
       when others die.
Perhaps we simply share the death
       with one we love.
Perhaps we take on the sorrowful moments
       as practice for ours.
Maybe we weep in gladness
       because we've been passed by;
or somehow we've felt the possibilities
       that we had so often ignored.

LEGACY

Let's talk about legacies –
remembrances of a certain person ago
replete with all the fantasies,
the augmented ego, an imagined memento.

Who knows? There may be impressive numbers attending
arranged assembly in my memory.
Let there be even those pretending
sympathy with those who tell my story.

Friends from the past might be there
(whoever can still manage to walk),
and perhaps some who simply wish to hear
tear-laden relatives try to talk.

All the "he was"s and "a time when"s
will be spoken in somber tones,
and sometimes the mythic inventions
will move sentimental moans.

But my legacy will really be the awareness
of the irony of all the consternation –
that those present will see the spareness
of such empty concentration.

THE LOUDNESS OF THE LEAVING

The cloud billowing, rising upward
From the disturbed bottom of earth,
    All the greatness,
    All the madness,
Unlike a tornado touching downward,
    Churning and swirling,
Infant and elder,
Newborn and ancient,
Debris of houses and automobiles,
Even flying unflown airplanes,
Tearing down towers –
The rest is silence
At the time of dying.

MAIL

Beneath the request for assistance
to starving and naked children
living in desolate places in a gray world,
all shown in pain-filled photographs,
is an oversized postcard about cruising to exotic, sunlit beaches
where clothes can be tossed aside in pristine pleasure.

Under that is a single sheet with pictures of lush young bodies
and the guarantee that one can be stripped of unwanted fat
and a nubile and sensual physique restored
without suffering demanding diets.

And then there is a carefully-folded advertisement
showing a vibrator in a variety of soft colors
which fits comfortably and discreetly in one's hand,
offering personal and pleasurable
escape from stress.

MISCELLANEA II

Something smears the pictures in our coloring book.

Is it simply time that wears down the bearing
until the grinding begins,
tortures our patience
as the screeching becomes intolerable?

One has a lot more time to himself when the others leave,
like the need to breathe in after the last exhalation
or the empty glass after the last swallow
or the space left after an explosion.

How is it that we smeared paint on ourselves
as we were decorating our lives?

What we draw becomes part of us,
If we colored outside the lines
we do so indelibly.

There is nothing left to say or to do
except to wish to begin anew.

To wish the gnarled tree
return to its seed,
to enter the softness within
where it begins.

MISSING THE EARLY SHOW

At the beach, young teens pranced,

each in her three-small-patches bikini,

hoping for a pretended-unintended revealing ("oo-oops!")

or anxious unveiling by chosen voyeurs ("hey-y-y!").

In such early-adolescent "show and tell" years,

in another time more secretive than such near-naked frankness,

while a few did strive for more exposure

and a few others even sampled the thrilling softness,

I felt the stern, firm, fatherly voice

through a shadowed wooden grate

warn, warn of such sinful pursuits.

Now in gray dismay,

I would right that wrong.

MY TURN

Stepping down from the commuter train,

the crowd moves quickly along the platform,

almost running to the revolving doors into the terminal.

Caught in the rush of the crowd,

I approach the quick-turning doors

hoping to find a rhythm to my steps

so that I can step nimbly into the spinning.

Tapping a white cane, a man steps in front of me,

his ticking stick discovering the space in the doors

into which he steps smoothly, effortlessly.

I watch the moving doors

and wait for an opening.

Clumsily, I thrust myself into the turning

Around a half-circle, then stepping out.

Once inside the terminal, I catch sight of the blind man

already half-way down the escalator.

Editor's note: *My father liked to play with the visual structure of poems as much as the written structure. I am not sure which version of the poem that follows on the next two pages was his preferred version, but finding the differences in look and wordplay interesting, both are included.*

MYSTERIES

Mysteries contain their own histories

I discovered that what I just uncovered,

       what seemed new, someone already knew:

       specimens archeological,

       relics deemed theological,

       manuscripts considered historical.

       Even pre-writing statements rhetorical

       I've become the uncovered specimen

       once deemed theological mystery,

       a relic known as Everyman

       and thus rhetoric becomes history.

RESEARCH

Mysteries contain

their own histories.

I discovered that

what I just uncovered,

    what seemed new

        someone already knew:

    fragments archeological,

    relics deemed theological,

    even writings rhetorical

reveal a familiar specimen,

the droppings of Everyman.

NARRATIVES

We, pilgrims truly, on a curious journey

to our destined sacred places,

each would willingly tell his tale as we went,

not for art, but simply to please listeners.

Though we may dress our storied people in costumes of heroes or victims –

the veils or cloaks of those who dream or lust;

the robes or hoods of scholars or voyeurs;

though masked in their staged make-up,

in the powdered pale of the frail or the frightened,

in the rubescent cheeks of clowns or madmen,

we would insist each story tell the saga of one's true self.

But our fabled actors are merely adorned exteriors,

willing containers of what others might imagine we are,

anxious to reflect a stately substance, an imposing image;

eager to portray such pretended faces on an appropriate stage,

to hold enthralled those who would watch and listen:

      to cause laughter (mirth is our mother tongue),

      to create tears (anguish is our second language).

Occasional passers-by might stop, watch a moment,
hear a line or two of our strained dialogue,
then move on, their attention drifting to merchandise in the stalls,
to press for bargains, not bravado or pathos.

Others would stay a while,
grinning casual interest
or even quietly nodding agreement
as we happily puffed out birthday candles
or uncomfortably extinguished funeral tapers
and unobtrusively veiled remembered abuses
and quickly covered shameful cruelties.

Oh, there were stories we might have sung:
the ones we did not wish to tell,
the ones we had forgotten,
the ones that never occurred!
In the tales we chose to relate,
we hated ourselves and we forgave ourselves,
defending arrogant appetites, offering reasonable excuses.

We honored our scoundrels and shunned our heroes
and resurrected our dead as we buried our living.
We wept for the designated unfortunates
and killed all the authorized enemies.

As if riding ridiculous roller-coasters
and feeling obligatory thrills,
we shunned our grounded requirements
and their deeper demands.

Exhausted by supposed satisfactions,
we would finally arrive near the outskirts of wherever,
content in not noticing how far we had wandered.
Like rested beasts, we would awaken refreshed,
determined to continue our wending ways.

We would see the trees waving welcome to our passing procession,
and admiring hills humbly lowering their shoulders, easing our vistas.
The sun would shine brightly and the nighttime stars would sparkle,
and these signs would confirm our stories.

OH SAY CAN YOU SEE

Tell us, you up there on the top,
do you still insist, after all this time has passed,
that your power and your wealth
must be further increased
       so that,
            by the trickling of some drops
                over the brim of your full cup,
            there will be a better day for us below?

But no salutary drops have dribbled down.

        Our present darkness has no early light of dawn.
Our eyes and ears and our hopes and fears are dazed
        with spangled banners and star-striped parades,
           with the spirited songs and flattering speeches
              of your pretentious patriotism
that so proudly hails to us below – the "free" and the "brave" –
        a standard of unliving
        that we should love and die defending.

Editor's note: *The final verse in this poem is nearly identical to a verse in "A Hermit's Life with Others" (page 20). I am unsure if my father intended to replace one poem with the other. Both poems, I think, have enough unique aspects to stand as separate works.*

ON THE MORNING OF DEPARTURE

Sunlight on familiar objects

discovers their newness.

Sun-brightened faces

shine in their youngness.

What once seemed always there,

like moments caught by an old Kodak,

now promises what will come later.

Everything seems a golden beginning!

But arrangements for leaving have been made

– non-exchangeable, non-refundable –

and the shuttle will arrive momentarily.

OR NOT TO BE

It's difficult to imagine becoming a mere memory —

to be frequent or seldom, distant or close, reminding or near-forgotten —

a familiar presence appearing without summons —

a momentary suggestion of warm touch —

a quickly-fading feeling unretrievable;

to be a recalled moment from a turned-open album of yellowed photos —

to be a stone marker's lost letters, a name, worn by wind and rain.

ROLE

He was an actor.

I watched him perform.

I saw him pretend that he was someone else.

He was a kind of magician.

He made my old friend disappear

      and I believed in the stranger on stage,

      and I felt his agony.

Now he's unable to pretend.

He's become transformed,

      an actual stranger.

And I can feel his agony.

RUBRICS OF GRATITUDE

In the after-moments of an event,
blurred reminiscence limns mere outlines
      of what really happened,
simplifies images of what transpired,
softens closeness to who was there.
Such haloed focus seems to wrongly define the dreamer,
to locate him in a lighted circle,
to cause him to construct his self-importance.

But I have learned living lessons
      in the length of my time
that remind my recollection of its unreliable nature --
that set me among shadows
      and show my mistakes.

Such truth was told to me somehow
by someone somewhere,
a memory mostly lost
      except for the stern sound,
      the warning.

It might have happened when I, a wandering child,

discovered that I was accompanied by shadowy figures.

They resembled me, mimed my movements,

       returned my waved greetings,

       but they were quite different,

         not my duplicates.

Often one followed me,

sometimes one led.

At times one strode at my side.

It might have happened, among those moving shapes,

that I sensed a power, perhaps even a person --

     one much wiser than I --

whose presence drew me closer,

whose closeness was pulsing in me,

who peered into my emptiness,

       my wondering,

       my yearning,

and spoke:

       "Understand that you have been noticed,

         not that you have selected --

       that you have been welcomed,

         not that you have been praised --

that you have received,

not that you have given --
that you have been embraced,

not that you have grasped --
that you have been loved,

not that you have loved.

Without us, your wandering companions,

you would not have known your direction,

you would not have known your progress,

you would not have even moved.

Only when we left you standing under the beam

of the mid-day sun
did you know the glare of loneliness.
Only when we left you groping

in the sun-less darkness
did you wish for our return.
And when we were once again with you,
you could move on again,

(proud of your own determination!)."

And so I left the place where wisdom was

and continued on my journey.

Along the difficult path, I found others who would walk with me a while --

some for days,

some for years,

and I remarked how insignificant all the places,

all the events,

all the joy,

all the sorrow,

in all my companion-less noontimes and nighttimes.

Nor did I understand,

until very late in years,

that it was I who,

like a proper shadow,

followed my companions.

SCHLÄFT EIN LIED

A lullaby sleeps in all things

There dreams on and on

And the world raises on to sing

Meets you only the magical word.

A song sleeps in all things

And the world's eternal dreaming

Sings a welcome

To your magical presence.

SHOW BIZ

I want to be the spotlighted singer
in the movie, who belts out the last song,
anguished lyrics forced from a sweating face,
legs strutting out fervid, pounding measures,
a primeval stripping bare of my soul,
flinging open my arms at the song's end,
rhythmic shrugs wringing last drops of passion,
embracing everyone, holding them all
tightly within the drumming, pulsing beat,
because I know, I know, what they want most!

SIMULATION

Transferring her lost passions to her dog,
she strokes softly as she would her lover,
wishing such constancy in another,
such affectionate acceptance, such trust.

Presences we create in our despair
attempt to perform as we have dreamt them,
but, unable to define their purpose,
drift away through mists of separation.

How little we know the truth about us;
yet we attempt to explain our feelings,
our being, in terms we use for creatures
that, somehow, we offered obeisant space.

Hopeful, unaware of substitution,
they accept our disappointed loving.

SONNET ON AN OCCASIONAL VISIT

You haven't changed a bit; you're still the same.

You're up-beat, as always; your smile still glows.

You're as you were over a year ago,

with an aura in which age doesn't count,

full of real joy – justified happiness.

You show your usual stately image,

like a proud blossom announcing the sun,

a youthful, unbothered, unworried face,

a kind of maidenly expectation.

Such lasting loveliness cannot survive

unless it's nurtured with raspy nettles

and painful trials that scar one's existence –

the necessary cost of persistence,

of continuing despite the anguish.

STRIPPING LESSON

Lowering the loins
I unzipped the skin,
unbuttoned the bowels,
untied the intestines,

opened the organs,
laid bare the bones,
       rapping sharply on them,
       thinking they'd fall apart.

But the bones and sinews held together quite firmly
       as twigs do to their branches
       and branches to their thicker limbs.
It was obvious that they were as usable
       as before they were unwrapped:

A little tissue here and there,
various bladders, filters, tubing, wiring,
a little fleshing out,
fresh fluids, a jump start
and Bob's your uncle!

TIME FOR AN ANNIVERSARY

There was a time
when time together was a wish.

And there were times together
when time was never time enough.

And there were times when "never enough"
demanded there be a time to settle that.

Then there were the times that finally
provided time enough to live in a happy time.

And, in time, there came again a time
when there was never enough time

To parcel out the time in timely fashion,
to use the time to answer time's demands.

And, in all that time, there was never enough time
to settle back and enjoy the time

That became more limited, more precious time,
time to whisper together, and, in time,

To say to one another, "What a time we have had!"
And, "Let's take the time to have even more happy times!"

TREMORS

A Haiku

Words said long ago,

surprised, I speak once again.

Wind storms returning.

TURNING

Corporate helicopters twirled over
> my suburban evening
> disturbing the soft music
> from the CD playing in another room,

distracting me in my early evening chair,
pausing my martini,

reminding me of the remoteness
> of peoples' worlds
> where the sounds of rotors whirling
> is commonplace disturbance
> of bird sounds and wind whispers,

drowning the lively gushing of mountain streams,

erasing the timepiece-like trickles
> of long-loyal fountains,

rushing overwhelming motor sounds

    through the bargaining voices in street markets,

54

where the daily world is militarily muted

by the resonance of destruction.

UNHEARD

There are words that no one has ever heard.

In the passages from brain to tongue

there are languages left strewn

in the back alleys of thought.

There are moments

when we disallow the voice to speak.

Instead, it hums in the echoes of music.

VANISHING POINTS

There are times when a person
      leaves living:
occasional moments
in which another presence
seems to occupy his body –
a few seconds sensing
      speaking in a remembered voice,
      turning one's wrist familiarly,
      chuckling quietly, distinctively,
      tilting one's glance again, seemingly –
brief visits in a different tense, perhaps,
friendly "just stopping by, can't stay" intervals.

VIGIL

The old cat,

the mother,

the baby,

the son,

the wife,

all must have known

when I watched their half-open eyes,

that I was asking their permission

to watch them die.

VILLANELLE POUR MON AMOUR

The force of breaking away from myself
Is chafing against your tender caring –
Not my fears of your loving demands.

My heart is haunted by its own lurking fears,
A specter chained by its selfish constraints.
These force my breaking away from myself.

I pretend to struggle for my freedom
But am prone to hide in my shaded moans,
Not from my fears of your loving demands.

Like a creature shaken from its shelter,
unknown sounds and unaccustomed presence
sap the force that breaks away from myself.

But shedding stony bramble from my soul,
I shirk shadows from my own enclosure,
But none from fears of your loving demands.

I feel the warm peace of your love's calming
And grim, cold shudders cease in your sunshine
Forcefully broken away from myself,
I deny fearing your loving demands.

WILDFLOWERS RISING IN THE BONEYARD

An occasional thought ultimately quantified,
orgasmic drizzle finally personified,

not from inspired intending,
not preconceived extending
    (details creatively blending),

but accidental,
    incidental;
        happenstance,
            perchance!

A need for deliberation,
    reasoned explanation,
        comforting clarification --
            these were appended,
            never comprehended.
    Ignorance was amended;
        truth was pretended.

What wasn't understood.
    was judged to be good
    (one did what one could,
        in all likelihood).

Grant it's a random event,

       a strangely ordered movement

       that places us, at least to some extent,

       here with no evident intent.

But (hell!) we're here!

At least, let's persevere!

WITHOUT GRAVITY

We all use different definitions.
The best we can do is connect somehow,
    Either on the top
    Or on the bottom.
We're like pieces floating weightless in space
Sometimes trying to steer ourselves,
Sometimes just reaching out.

Sometimes we bump into one another
And sometimes we hold on for a while.

About the author

James Wicklund spent nearly 40 years in education as a teacher and administrator, largely in the northwest suburbs of Chicago. Writing poetry for most of his adult life, he published his first collection of poems, *Notes Found Scratched on a Bald Spot*, in 2010. James died in 2020, leaving behind loving family members, friends, colleagues and decades of previously unpublished poetry. You can find an expanding archive of that work at **jameswicklund.com**.